IMAGES
of England

AROUND
RAWMARSH
AND PARKGATE

Tram 14 of the Mexborough and Swinton Tramway Company lying in gardens at the foot of old Warren Vale following an accident on 30 July 1908. The workmen's car from Rotherham had been full of colliers travelling to work when it ran out of control and jumped the points. Twenty-one passengers were injured in all but fortunately none suffered worse than a broken nose. In the 1920s the steep gradient of old Warren Vale was a major concern of the Board of Trade with regard to tram operation.

IMAGES
of England

AROUND
RAWMARSH
AND PARKGATE

Anthony Dodsworth

TEMPUS

A drawing of the old St Mary's church, just before it was taken down in 1838. This is the only surviving view of what the old church looked like. Virtually none of this church survives apart from some remnants of a Norman doorway. Earl Fitzwilliam laid the first stone of the new church that, it is recorded, was dedicated to St Lawrence. This dedication was presumably changed at a later date. As with many churches in the area its lofty elevation makes it highly visible over a large area.

First published 2002, reprinted 2003

Tempus Publishing Limited
The Mill, Brimscombe Port,
Stroud, Gloucestershire, GL5 2QG

British Library Cataloguing in Publication Data.
A catalogue record for this book is available from the British Library.

ISBN 0 7524 2495 5

Typesetting and origination by Tempus Publishing Limited
Printed in Great Britain by Midway Colour Print, Wiltshire

Contents

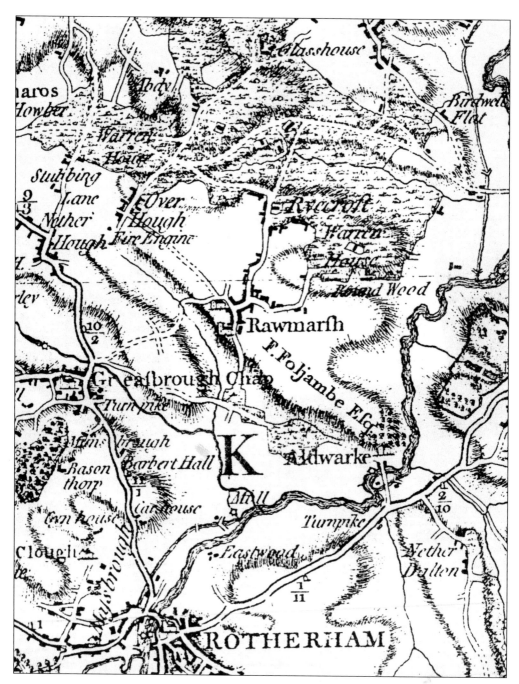

Thomas Jeffery's map of the West Riding of Yorkshire 1767-1771. The village of Rawmarsh is clustered around High Street, Stocks Lane, Dale Road and Green Lane with St Mary's church and Rawmarsh Hall shown separately. Parkgate appears not to exist as a settlement but Aldwarke Hall and Aldwarke water mill on the River Don are shown. Isolated squatter homesteads and tofts can be seen on the common to the north and a tantalising glimpse of the early development of coal mining is indicated by a Fire Engine named at Over Hough (Upper Haugh). Both Warren Houses are named and reflect the significance of rearing rabbits that continued well into the eighteenth century.

Introduction

Rawmarsh and Parkgate are found close to the large town of Rotherham in South Yorkshire having grown together over the past 150 years. Despite their close proximity these two settlements have sharply contrasting histories. Rawmarsh has a long and well documented history with a reference in the Domesday Book and a church that stylistically dated back to Norman times. This church building was demolished in 1839 and replaced by a Victorian successor on the same site near the top of Rawmarsh Hill. Within this church, St Mary's, a cross shaft and base of twelfth-century origin is preserved and the list of named rectors stretches back to William De Sutton in 1227. In contrast the great majority of Parkgate's history stretches no further back than 1823 when two Sheffield men, Sanderson and Watson, established an ironworks there. It is the iron, and later the steel, industry that has been the proud focus of Parkgate's identity up to the present day with the huge works that comprise the Aldwarke, Roundwood and Thrybergh sites still operating. The name Parkeyeate is first recorded in a will dated 1559 and most likely referred to the area beside the emparked area that surrounded Aldwarke Hall.

The oldest visible feature of Rawmarsh's past is Roman Ridge which forms a significant part of the western boundary of the parish. This linear bank and ditch feature stretches intermittently through several miles of South Yorkshire and has puzzled antiquarians and archaeologists alike for centuries. In the distant past it was considered to be a Roman road (hence its erroneous title) but in more recent times it has been tentatively recognised as a tribal boundary marker dating back to early in the Dark Ages. Few settlements in England can have been referred to by such a variety of place-names as Rawmarsh. The earliest record of 1086 refers to Rodemesc, followed by Rubeo Marisco in 1239, Routhemersk in 1293 and Romerssh in 1441. The origins of the name Rawmarsh are always a topic of lively discussion in the area as is the way it should be pronounced. Only distant visitors actually pronounce it as it is spelt. Those more familiar refer to 'Row-marsh' while long-established locals insist on 'Ro-mish', which is interesting considering its form in 1441.

The two most notable secular buildings in the Rawmarsh and Parkgate area, Aldwarke Hall and Rawmarsh Hall, have long since disappeared, as have the houses which served the three manors that divided up the parish in medieval times. One manor house was sited in the centre of Rawmarsh village close to the parish church of St Mary's, with another to the east at Wheatcroft and the third to the west at Stubbin. The manor based at Stubbin was controlled by the Vicars Choral of the Collegiate Church of St Mary, Southwell, for centuries and much of the early written history of at least part of Rawmarsh can be found in their records. Here are references to the original ownership of the Deyncourt family and to more quirky details such as ground rents paid with money and payments in kind – 'armis porcubus' or 'with flitches of bacon'! Even from as early as the fifteenth century detailed references are made to the existence and exploitation of coal reserves in the area. This was a forerunner of much more systematic exploitation of coal in the Rawmarsh and Parkgate area from the early eighteenth century onwards. This largely shaped the more recent history of the area and perhaps provided the driving force behind the enclosure of the common fields and common lands of Rawmarsh in 1781.

The exploitation of the agricultural potential of the lands around Rawmarsh village and its outlying hamlets of Stubbin and Upper Haugh was obviously a key feature of the area's economy from Domesday times down to the end of the eighteenth century and this can be traced by reference to wills and probate inventories from this period. However profound changes had already occurred within the parish by the time of the census of 1811, for even this early a majority of the heads of household were involved in non-agricultural work. Coal mining accounted for some of this but the area was also noted for its pottery industry and, from as early as the beginning of the eighteenth century, the Hallam family were closely linked to the industry. They helped to establish Low Pottery between High Street and Dale Road and later in the century the Hawleys set up Top Pottery just 300 yards away. In the nineteenth century Meadow Pottery was built to the east of Claypit Lane and there is evidence of more pot making in other areas of the parish such as at Warren Vale. None was as famous as the Rockingham Pottery easily visible across Rawmarsh's northern boundary but all contributed to the industrialization of the village and its workforce as the nineteenth century progressed.

For most of the seventeenth and eighteenth centuries it was the Foljambe family established at Aldwarke Hall that dominated the economic development of Rawmarsh, but as the nineteenth century progressed the Fitzwilliam family from nearby Wentworth Woodhouse became more and more involved being especially important in exploiting the coal resources. It was this developing coal industry in Rawmarsh that saw the settlement experience quite rapid population growth in the second half of the nineteenth century.

Meanwhile the growth of Parkgate from 1823 was nothing short of explosive. From being a tiny satellite of the village of Rawmarsh, Parkgate grew so quickly that it rapidly overhauled Rawmarsh. From its original site, west of the main Rotherham road, the ironworks moved east to beside the London, Midland and Scottish Railway line in the 1860s to benefit from the improved communications. Typical of most heavy industries from this time the fortunes of the iron, and later, steel works in Parkgate fluctuated, experiencing an economic roller-coaster ride but the good times were very good indeed with the period 1856 to 1861 seeing the Parkgate works as the only one in the country capable of producing huge rolled armour plate for naval ships. Workers flocked in from all over the country but especially from iron-producing counties like Staffordshire.

The housing around the ironworks grew at an extraordinary rate, sometimes financed by the workers themselves through organisations such as temperance groups. Tradesmen and shopkeepers were attracted to serve this burgeoning community and Broad Street and Rawmarsh Hill developed as the main commercial thoroughfare in the area. Comparative stagnation in the area in the latter part of the twentieth century has meant that most of the buildings lining Broad Street and Rawmarsh Hill have survived intact and photographs taken right at the beginning of the twentieth century remain fascinatingly similar to photographs taken in the year 2000 save for the clothes of the people shown and for the vehicles on the road itself. Work in the iron and steel works has always been physically exacting but the local people of Parkgate have always taken great pride in their capabilities. The opening of Victoria Park at Rosehill in 1901 and the building of the Carnegie Library on Rawmarsh Hill in 1904 were both occasions for immense civic pride in Rawmarsh as was the opening of the town's own swimming baths in 1927. Under no circumstances did local inhabitants see Rawmarsh as a suburb of Rotherham instead they saw Rotherham as almost a civic competitor. When Mr J. Spick, Chairman of Rawmarsh Urban District Council, received the swimming baths and concert hall on Saturday 5 November 1927 on behalf of the council he could not resist including in his speech 'We had sewage works before Rotherham; we had a steam roller before Rotherham; we have a park worth two of Rotherham's...' for the people of Rawmarsh took pride in their home town and, despite the many changes, still do so today. In many ways the photographs in this book reflect the pride of the past and present inhabitants of Rawmarsh and Parkgate in their home towns.

One

Out and About

Looking down Rawmarsh Hill towards the centre of Parkgate, *c.* 1908. On the left is a row of stone cottages. These were marked on the Tithe Map of 1848 and called Stone Row when they stood in splendid isolation in the no-man's land between Parkgate and Rawmarsh. Over the next half century the rapid growth of Parkgate saw both sides of Rawmarsh Hill completely built up. Stone Row is one of the few parts of Broad Street and Rawmarsh Hill that was demolished during the twentieth century. Otherwise the view along the main thoroughfare through Parkgate is remarkably unaltered since the early years of the century. Most of the housing in Parkgate was brick built (even if sometimes faced in stone) so these cottages were comparatively unusual locally.

Stocks Lane, Rawmarsh, after 1910 when the overhead wires had been installed for the Swinton and Mexborough trams. There is no need to mention what the little boy on the right may be shovelling from the road! Despite the presence of some old and clearly historic buildings in the lane this whole area was cleared for redevelopment in the late 1960s.

This prospect of St Mary's church shows one of the ponds close to Westfield Road in the foreground, c. 1895. It is one of the most popular views of the parish church. The pond may have been linked to the small colliery that operated nearby in the nineteenth century.

10

The cottage that can be seen standing up on the left when descending Warren Vale, c. 1950. On the 1740 Fairbanks map of Rawmarsh Common it was shown as being occupied by William Padley, a collier born in Tankersley. Later it was associated with the Carr and Scholefield families. Recently two pottery kilns were discovered in the cottage walls.

The top end of Dale Road as it rises to Lane Head, c. 1920. The cart with the churns climbing the hill is a reminder of the area's farming links.

Rosehill Hall was built around 1800 of stone quarried, it is said, locally from Darfield and Hooton Roberts. Its surviving cellars are hewn out of solid rock. During the First World War it was used to house Belgian refugees.

The church and school of Christ Church close to Four Lane Ends, Parkgate, *c.* 1914. The church was built in 1868 to cater for the explosive expansion of Parkgate that saw it outgrow its neighbour Rawmarsh in the later part of the nineteenth century. The church was demolished in 1961.

A row of terraced houses in Green Lane, Rawmarsh around the time of the First World War. Note that at this time the roadway had not yet been properly surfaced. The entrance to Green Lane Farm would have been a little further up the road on the opposite side. The houses have bay windows and narrow front gardens, both key features of the better terraced houses built around 1900. The open space beyond the last terraced house was to be filled by the 1950s with St Joseph's, a new Catholic church and primary school.

Aldwarke Hall towards the end of the nineteenth century, not long before its demolition in 1899. This building was completed for Francis Foljambe around 1720 and replaced a long, low and many gabled house. Aldwarke had been associated with several important families in medieval times such as the Clarels and the Fitzwilliams. This house was an H-shaped stone building in a plain classical style. No trace survives today as the site is now occupied by the Aldwarke Melting Shops.

The South Yorkshire and River Don Navigation near Rotherham Road, Parkgate, c. 1900. This canal, with a spur to Cinder Bridge at Greasbrough, had played a vital role in the early development of coal mining in the area. It is easy to see its importance had diminished by 1900 due to the increasing use of rail transport for coal.

Two of the terraced houses on Rawmarsh Hill in 1912. The people are waiting to see King George V and Queen Mary who travelled through Parkgate on their visit to a number of local collieries.

Originally erected as the Rawmarsh Wesleyan church on High Street close to Rawmarsh Hall, this building is more often remembered as Robbie's Picture Palace. It was built in the 1870s to replace an old chapel that was pulled down. Services continued in the Star Inn club house while this church was being built. It was replaced by the existing Methodist church on High Street in 1908.

A wall monument commemorating Francis Foljambe, Esquire, and found in Ecclesfield church. He was lord of the manors of Rawmarsh and Wheatcroft and lived at Aldwarke Hall. Aldwarke has a very complicated history because for many centuries it has been a detached portion of the parish of Ecclesfield, hence the location of the monument there. On his monument Francis is referred to as 'a kind landlord and an indulgent Master'. He died in December 1752.

Old Warren Vale looking towards the woods on the skyline that today are near the Woodman Roundabout. A tram slowly climbs the steep gradient of Warren Vale, around 1908. Concern about the gradient, and two serious tram accidents, eventually led to a new route for Warren Vale being constructed in the late 1920s.

Joan Ratcliffe and Eileen Concannon lead their children up Netherfield Lane close to the primary school in 1949. Mary Ratcliffe is on the left with Yvonne Concannon and Nora Ratcliffe in the pushchair. A friend, Anne Stitch, accompanies them.

The old Queen's Hotel on Kilnhurst Road, *c.* 1900. It was replaced soon afterwards by the existing building despite being less than forty years old when demolished. The sign above the door shows William Cope to be the landlord. He was also a farmer of land in Greasbrough parish.

Part of Roman Ridge close to the hamlet of Hoober. This is the oldest visible landscape feature in the Rawmarsh area although it is more likely to date from the early part of the Dark Ages than from Roman times. Consisting, even today, of a very clear bank and ditch Roman Ridge forms much of the north-west boundary of the parish of Rawmarsh.

A classic view of Rawmarsh Hill, *c.* 1914. Amazingly the original view was printed as a postcard in reverse so it probably did not sell very well! Close to this point, in January 1926 William Ward (aged eight) was knocked down and killed by a car. He had rushed into the road without looking while chasing an ambulance car.

Rosehill Hall and the marble drinking fountain. The Hall was long associated with the Firth family who finally left the property some time between 1845 and 1849. Over the next fifty years it had a number of occupiers including the Reverend Sir William Ross Mahon, rector of the parish church for many years. At the time of Queen Victoria's Diamond Jubilee in 1897 it was suggested that the occasion be marked locally by the provision of a public park. The park and house were bought and opened as Victoria Park on Whit Monday in May 1901. A further embellishment, a marble drinking fountain, was added in 1903 to commemorate the coronation of Edward VII.

Rosehill (Victoria) Park in its heyday before the First World War. This view is apparently from upstairs in the Hall. The terraced houses of Queen Street can be seen in the distance.

Rosehill Park's Bowling Green, c. 1913. The park developed a full range of leisure facilities over the years including a tennis court, two aviaries, a paddling pool and a bandstand, which opened in 1931. Councillor Hutchinson is seen here standing on the bowling surface. He was involved in the opening of the bowling pavilion.

Cottages on Blackamoor Road on the northern parish boundary between Rawmarsh and Swinton. A building was marked here on the 1740 map of Rawmarsh Common and was then occupied by John Bayley, a collier. On the 1855 Ordnance Survey map it is named as Blackamoor Inn. The sharp bend in the road outside the cottages is a typical feature found on a parish boundary.

Parkgate and Aldwarke Station on the Great Central Railway, c. 1904. The station featured in a Diana Dors film *Tread Softly Stranger*, shot in the 1950s.

A 1920s sketch of Pipe House by Percy Caroline. The local Pipe House Lane next to Rosehill Park is obviously named after this building. It is shown on the earliest map of the area produced by William Fairbanks in 1740. The area was associated with the Scorah family from the seventeenth century until well into the nineteenth century. They used the local supply of suitable clay from the adjoining Rawmarsh Common to produce clay pipes, a business they were associated with for at least 150 years. Not far away beyond Rawmarsh Common, and over the parish boundary with Swinton, the Rockingham Pottery exploited the same area to produce its world-famous pottery.

Broad Street in the mid-1920s, looking towards Rawmarsh Hill and the heart of Parkgate. The name Parkgate is first recorded in a will of 1559 and is likely to refer to a gate to Aldwarke Hall that lay nearby.

23

Kilnhurst Road at Ryecroft where North Street joins the main road, *c.* 1910. The Queen's Hotel can be seen in the distance. In medieval times a farm, Ryecroft, had been established in the area probably incorporating land that was originally part of Rawmarsh Common. The farm continued operating into the twentieth century. The area began to be developed for housing from the 1870s with a New Freehold Land Society being set up on 15 November 1873. The initial meeting at the Star Inn heard of the district's 'abundant water supply' and of it being 'healthy and fertile with good roads'! Local notables such as George Hawley, Samuel Ainley, Richard Hicks and T.W. Roome were on the first committee.

This Congregational church was built in Stocks Lane and opened in March 1888. It cost over £1,250 to build. The 'Congs' Sunday school was found to the rear close to the yard of Scales' butchers shop in Dale Road.

A Swinton and Mexborough tram toils up the old Warren Vale road in the late 1900s. The cottages in the distance can still be seen today. The liberating effects of bicycles for women is hinted at in the foreground and the raised umbrella on the tram's upper deck suggests strong sunshine rather than rain!

A small crowd pose for the camera in Upper Haugh on the unmade road that is now Green Rise, *c.* 1910. Shaw's farm is shown on the left with Hobson's farm on the right.

A trolley bus waiting at the bottom of Bear Tree Road, Parkgate *c.* 1960. Not long after this trolley buses were phased out.

Almshouses in Dale Road, pictured some time before 1892 – the year that they were pulled down. The five new ones that were built to replace them have also gone now. The almshouses were financed by the Goodwin family who at one time lived in Rawmarsh Hall. The shadowy building in the background is the old boys' grammar school.

The organ inside the Methodist chapel in Upper Haugh that was demolished in the 1980s. The chapel had been built in 1879 at the cost of £1,500. Elsie May Beaumont was the organist here for many years and recalls the Backhouse family from Upper Haugh who were well known for their singing as a family. The father of the family was known as 'Holy Joe' because he was a local preacher.

The chapel in Rawmarsh New Cemetery in Haugh Road as it appeared on its opening in 1908. This building, made up of an Anglican and a Non-Conformist chapel, was consecrated by the Bishop of Sheffield. The rapid growth of the local population led to extreme pressure on burial space in the area. The High Street cemetery had been extended in 1880 but still proved inadequate by the early 1900s. The new cemetery was over ten acres in size and had 9,000 grave spaces.

Opposite, bottom: Aldwarke House to the left of the lock gates on the River Don Navigation, *c.* 1900. Aldwarke House was the home of the Oxley family, the renowned Parkgate steelworks owners, for many years. The lock was required to enable barges to get past the weir on the river.

Rosehill Park was used as the centre of a 'Holidays at Home' scheme that began during the Second World War and continued to the 1950s. The scheme was immensely popular with local children, some even foregoing holidays at the seaside so they could take part.

The war memorial near the top of Rawmarsh Hill. Close to it is buried 'The Little Cross' that preceded it in somewhat controversial circumstances. Formerly the site had been occupied by the village pinfold and more recently by a men's urinal.

Gooseholes just before its demolition, c. 1938. These two old cottages had a prominent position on Haugh Road near Upper Haugh. Their name is supposedly linked to a nearby pond with a resident flock of geese. The cottages were last occupied by Joe Carr and the Backhouse family, both closely linked with Upper Haugh Methodist chapel.

Rawmarsh Free Library on Rawmarsh Hill not long after its official opening in 1905. It was largely funded by Andrew Carnegie, an American benefactor who financed the building of many public libraries in this country. The library was diplomatically sited close to the junction of Rawmarsh and Parkgate and so avoided the controversy that surrounded the siting of the swimming baths later in the century.

St Mary's church at the top of Rawmarsh Hill, *c.* 1904. Set just below the church (close to the location of the war memorial) was the village pinfold where stray animals were held in the past. William Vesey Ross Mahon had been rector at the church from 1844 to 1893. He divided his time between Rawmarsh and his ancestral home at Strokestown, Roscommon in Ireland.

Four Lane Ends, Parkgate, at the time of the First World War. The Travellers' Inn, seen on the left, still serves the area today.

An entrance to Aldwarke Hall off Aldwarke Lane, late in the nineteenth century. The Hall was demolished in 1899 but the associated farm, stables buildings and entrance survived well into the twentieth century.

The hamlet of Upper Haugh, *c.* 1910. Originally dominated by large farms such as Manor Farm, more and more coal miners settled here as the nineteenth century progressed because of the proximity to the Old Stubbin pit.

A rare view of the developing area of Ryecroft from the south, early in the twentieth century. Looking across the valley of Roundwood Brook behind the tram sheds, the terraced streets of Ryecroft, Main Street and South Street, can be seen. New Dale Colliery operated close to this point but the colliery company went into liquidation in 1897.

Bassett Cottage, c. 1900. The cottage was situated in quite an isolated location west of the centre of Rawmarsh village beside the Low Stubbin Incline. It was traditionally the home of the under manager of Stubbin Colliery. The Walker family lived here in the 1930s but the cottage was occupied by Gad Hollings around the time of this photograph.

The almshouses built in 1892 to house poor women of the local area. The Goodwin family that provided the investments for these cottages had first come to Rawmarsh in 1577 when Anthony Goodwin was appointed as rector. Selling mining rights under some of the Goodwin Trust estate in Greasbrough helped finance the almhouses.

A cottage on Chapel Walk, Upper Haugh, close to the stone path that ran out of the southern end of the little settlement and across the Stubbin Incline that carried coal down towards the River Don. This view of around 1900 shows the Dyson family outside the front door. Harry Beaumont's father recalled going there when he was six or seven to scrub the stone floors.

Two

High Street, Rawmarsh:
Heart of the Village

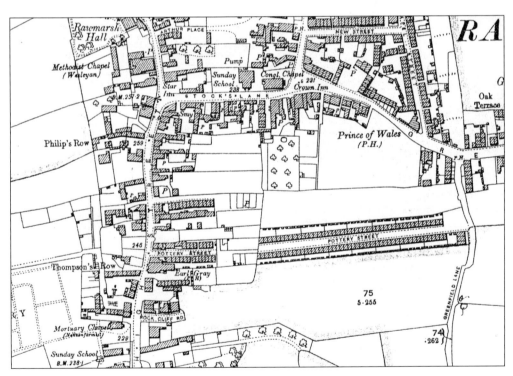

High Street, Rawmarsh as shown on the Ordnance Survey 1:2500 map published in 1903. Nearly all the small terraces leading off the High Street have now disappeared and Pottery Street has ceased to exist. The large building at the northern end of the High Street was Rawmarsh Hall, then occupied by the Knapton family, but later demolished and replaced by the swimming baths. A few remnants of 'old' Rawmarsh as seen here have survived into the twenty-first century.

A sketch of the existing Methodist church on High Street by W.J. Hale of Sheffield, the architect. The foundation stones of the new church were laid on Easter Monday, 1907 but the land used had been bought partly in 1894 from Mr Foljambe and partly in 1902 from Earl Fitzwilliam. A meeting in 1898 to discuss a new church led to promises of £541 towards the building costs; an impressive figure.

Providence Place, c. 1965. This was one of a number of yards that opened on to High Street. The outlook to the east was still quite open.

High Street close to the top of Pottery Street as it looked in the 1900s. The Earl Grey Inn shown here had Joseph Hicks as landlord in 1879. The Hicks were a notable Rawmarsh family throughout the nineteenth and into the twentieth century. It was here that the Rawmarsh, Parkgate and District Cow Club met with Henry Hicks as the secretary. Members paid 3s 6d for every cow they owned and if a cow died or was killed the owner received £12. Apparently it was a Victorian animal accident insurance policy!

High Street before the tramlines were laid in 1906. The roof of the old Methodist chapel can be seen in the distance where, following its conversion to a cinema, Mrs Robinson kept order in the 'cheap seats' with a very long cane. The 'Penny Rush' is remembered by many local people, although even a two pound jam jar might gain you entry if you had no money at all.

A trolley bus of the Mexborough and Swinton Traction Company parked on Dale Road outside the tram sheds. This is shortly before the closure of the trolley bus system in 1961.

The old Rectory that stands opposite St Mary's church and is now disused. Christopher Stephenson, the rector, records that the foundation for the building was laid in June 1752. Parish records note that in 1797 thirteen new sash windows were put in.

The Regal Picture House on High Street as it appeared in the 1950s. It originally opened in October 1931 and provided a more comfortable film watching experience than that to be had at 'Robbie's' across the road. The building has been used more recently as a supermarket.

The Rawmarsh Baths and Concert Hall on Haugh Road were opened in November 1927 by Earl Fitzwilliam. The building was demolished in 2001. It consisted of a bathing pool measuring 75 feet by 35 feet. For concert and dance purposes a special oak sprung floor covered the pool. The possibility of Rawmarsh having its own swimming baths was first raised in the 1880s and by 1907 it was quite usual for candidates at local elections to advocate 'baths for Rawmarsh'. The Haugh Road site was finally chosen in preference to others put forward in France Street and Westfield Road. The land was provided by Earl Fitzwilliam on the understanding that miners at the end of their shifts could shower or bathe in the building.

A performance of the Rawmarsh and Parkgate Choral Society in the Rawmarsh Baths Hall not long after it opened in 1927. The Choral Society began originally in 1873 under the title of the Sacred Harmonic Society. Thomas Brameld was one of the principal movers in its creation.

A sketch of Thomas Brameld who was born in a cottage in Green Lane, Rawmarsh, in 1848. He was central to the development of a number of local musical, choral and instrumental societies from the 1870s until his death in 1915. He came from a musical background, his grandfather, Thomas Wilson had on one occasion walked from Rawmarsh to York to sing at the Minster! By 1869 he was giving music lessons and these continued at his home, 73 Rawmarsh Hill. His work with the Rawmarsh and Parkgate Sacred Harmonic Society achieved local recognition and he went on to considerable success with music societies in Doncaster, Ecclesfield and Rotherham. Towards the end of his life he attended the Leeds Festival Dinner at which Sir Edward Elgar was the principal guest. After the speeches Brameld was pointed out to Elgar who responded 'Yes, I have heard about him, do please introduce me to him'.

The Les Barnes Band performing at Rawmarsh Baths in its 'dance hall mode' in 1951. Many acquaintances made here on the dance floor led later to romance and marriage for the people of Rawmarsh and Parkgate.

Above: Rawmarsh Hall, early in the twentieth century. This large house was originally associated with the Goodwin family who moved into Rawmarsh from East Grinstead in Sussex in the latter part of the sixteenth century. The house stood on the corner of Haugh Road on the land occupied later by the swimming baths. It was occupied by the Knapton family shortly before its demolition.

Opposite: The Rawmarsh Band with conductor Mr Ackroyd in the grounds of Rawmarsh Hall in 1921. The band members include Herbert Simpson, Bill Roebuck and John Painter. They used to practice in a building behind the Star Inn in Stocks Lane.

Brian and Irene Lilley and a friend pose on a motorbike, *c.* 1935. They are by Lilley's Yard on High Street and across the road can be seen Fowler's hairdressers, Marsh's cobblers and a sweet shop. The house was occupied by another member of the Lilley family, John Willey Lilley, an insurance agent. The entrance to the Council Yard was beside his house.

Rawmarsh High Street close to its junction with Stocks Lane a few years before the tram tracks were laid in 1906. A gas lamp stands outside Ward's fruit shop with an elegantly attired Edith Mary Ward posing at its entrance.

Parkin's wool and haberdashery shop at the end of Philip's Row, c. 1965. Miss Holroyd had run the shop before the Parkins and early in the century it had been the site of Henry Hicks' saddlery business. The building is still standing but shortened as a result of road widening.

The old building in the High Street that houses Clark's undertaking business, c. 1965. This is probably the oldest surviving building in the High Street. The Clark family have operated a joiner/undertaker and wheelwright business from here since 1784. Two large parish ovens are believed to still exist behind one of the interior walls.

Favell's grocers shop and off licence was in High Street opposite Ward's fruit shop and across from the top of Stocks Lane. The advertisements for Kellogg's Rice Krispies, Tetley's beer, Robinson's lemon barley drink, Senior Service cigarettes and Cherry Blossom polish recall the post-war years. The Favells took over the shop from the Locketts in the mid-1930s.

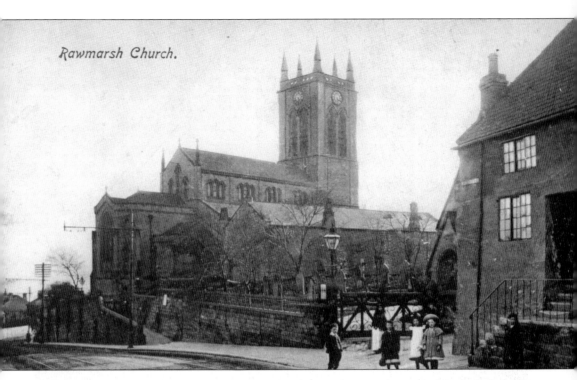

Rawmarsh Church.

Above: St Mary's, the parish church of Rawmarsh, standing at the top of Rawmarsh Hill, c. 1900. The church hall built beside it served as the infants department of Dale Road school at about this time. The house with the steps on the right is an old building referred to in documents relating to the Rawmarsh Enclosure Award of 1781 as the homestead and malt office of Matthew Blacksmith. Matthew lived here with his wife, Ann Slack, whom he had married in 1779.

Opposite: The old Earl Grey Inn was demolished and replaced by a new building in 1957. The building shown here was first mentioned as an inn in an 1833 directory but its massive wooden frame and low ceilings suggested it was older still. In 1858 it had a stable, cowhouse and cart shed at the back alongside the buildings of Top Pottery.

Samuel, a coal miner, and Christiana Sellars pose outside their cottage just off the High Street in the entrance to the Council Yard, c. 1900. The small porch seems to have been a popular design for several houses in the centre of Rawmarsh are shown with them and a couple of them still survive.

Above: The Manor House on High Street, Rawmarsh was demolished with much of the heart of the village in the road widening scheme of the 1960s. It was here that the Foljambes usually held their manorial courts. A king post was uncovered during its demolition, a sign of its previous high status.

The No. 18 Mexborough and Swinton tram passes along High Street, c. 1915. The spire of the relatively new Methodist church can be seen in the background. A tramway between Rotherham and Rawmarsh was first proposed in 1877 but was met with a storm of protest from Rawmarsh tradesmen who feared that local people would go into Rotherham for shopping.

A crowd throngs across the High Street near St Mary's church, c. 1910. In June 1808 a meeting was held at the Star Inn nearby to consider applying to Parliament to make a turnpike road between Rotherham and Rawmarsh and then on to Swinton.

High Street looking towards St Mary's church, *c.* 1955. Ward's greengrocery business is on the left on the corner with Stocks Lane.

Sunnyside Cottage, High Street with the Ward family standing outside, *c.* 1902. Tom Ward sits in the middle with, left to right behind him, Albert Ward, his wife Edith Mary and George Ward. Tom and Edith's daughters, Mary and Dorothy, are in front of Tom. This cottage is also known as Dame Hawley's Cottage and was once occupied by a widow of the Hawley family, who operated several local potteries. Dame Hawley lived here with her two nieces. The location of the cottage set back from the edge of High Street is easily picked out on the Rawmarsh Tithe Map of the 1840s and saved it from destruction when the High Street was widened.

A Mexborough and Swinton tram standing outside the old Manor House on High Street, c. 1908. The post office can be seen opposite the Manor House with the Star Inn in the background. The aproned figure may be Henry Hicks standing outside his saddlery business. In 1879 he had been honorary secretary of the Rawmarsh, Parkgate and District Cow Club.

A very old building on the High Street, c. 1900. Twenty years earlier a joiner called James Ludlam had lived here or very close by. His dog was reputedly so lazy that it lay down to bark. This is said to have given rise to the local saying 'as idle as Ludlam's dog'.

A wedding group including the bridegroom Horace Espley and his new wife Edith Lilley, c. 1925. They pose outside 18 High Street, the home of John W. Lilley. Left to right, back row: Richard Lowe, Gissie Barwick, Sam Lilley, Edith Lilley, Florrie Rowbotham, Eunice Bennett. Middle row includes John Lilley, ? Shirtcliffe, Alice Lilley, Revd and Mrs Scott Jones, Ernest Lilley, Lily Davies, James Johnson, Bertha Johnson, Ada Lilley, George Lilley, Arthur Wray (Snr). Front row includes Polly Jones (seated left), Athur Jones, Eliza Lilley (seated right), Ginny Wray and Arthur Wray (Jnr).

Thomas Steel standing outside his home at 5 Arthur Place close to the centre of Rawmarsh. He was born in 1827 and died in 1903, a few years after this picture. For much of his life he worked for the Knapton Family at Rawmarsh Hall across the High Street. He was particularly responsible for the horses.

Three

A Hive of Industry

The whole of the Park Gate steelworks and surrounding area from the air, c. 1960. The extent to which the old steelworks (demolished in the 1970s) dominated the settlement of Parkgate is easily appreciated here. In 1963 secret plans for a proposed air raid by German bombers were uncovered. The attack, to hit strategic points in the steelworks, was planned as early as October 1939 but never materialised. The pilots were told to follow the River Don and warned of anti-aircraft posts at Rotherham and Chesterfield. The Park Gate works played a crucial role in the Second World War particularly linked to its production of armour plating for shipping.

EDUCATION
and a
CAREER in ONE

PARK GATE STEEL is everywhere around you in everyday life—reliable and of the highest reputation.

All this depends on people who have practised and studied one of the score of separate methods, skills and sciences which make up the undoubted success of **PARK GATE**.

Continued success depends on recruitment, training, and the further education of young people.

When a young man joins **PARK GATE** he gets every opportunity to learn about iron and steel processing, to get the widest possible experience and to attend college for vocational studies.

If you are interested in iron and steel manufacture or commerce or engineering or metallurgy or associated technical experience please write or call.

THE PARK GATE IRON & STEEL
COMPANY LIMITED, ROTHERHAM

A ⓣ Company   TELEPHONE: ROTHERHAM 2141 (10 lines)

TELEGRAMS: YORKSHIRE, PARKGATE, YORKS.   •   TELEX 54141

This advert appeared regularly in the Rawmarsh Urban District Council Handbook in the 1950s and emphasized the key role the iron and steelworks played in the life of the local community.

Molten steel inside the 24 inch Section Mill at the heart of the Park Gate iron and steelworks, c. 1923. Increased mechanisation reduced the number of very dangerous jobs in the works. In 1860 puddlers, shinglers and hammermen performed extremely demanding and dangerous manual tasks every day.

The steelworks were vital to the country's war effort between 1939 and 1945 and women were needed for some of the jobs involved. Practically every British large bomber aircraft on active service in the Second World War relied on Parkgate cold pressed plates for their brake drums.

The chemical works that were located on Taylor's Lane close to Mangham. Large quantities of local coal were transformed here into material such as coke, benzol and road tar. Shown here in full production in 1936 they closed in 1975 and were demolished.

A view of the site of the Park Gate ironworks developed east of the Rotherham–Rawmarsh road, c. 1865. The original ironworks developed west of the main road and adjoining Taylor's Lane from 1823. It was relocated in the 1860s to benefit from a larger site and a location alongside the London-Midland-Scottish railway line.

J. Cartwright, F. Underhay and J. Evans worked in mines drainage and are seen here at the Kilnhurst shaft in 1973. F. Underhay wears some of the specialist clothing that is more reminiscent of Samurai warriors!

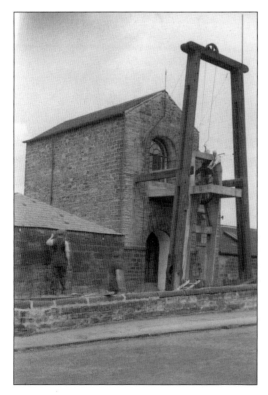

The engine house on Westfield Road, Parkgate, c. 1937. This is one of the few surviving remnants of the coal industry that was once so important locally. The mines drainage unit was based here at one time.

Above: A group of steelworkers from the Park Gate works, *c.* 1900. The young lad sitting in front of the group is one of the Small family. He began work there aged twelve. Initially he worked as a glazier under his father but eventually he became a roller until the old No. 2 mill was dismantled and sent off to Spain. Much of the work in the iron and steel works was very arduous and highly skilled. A variety of specialised trades involving puddlers, rollers, shinglers and furnacemen were found in the works. In the second half of the nineteenth century some of these workers were closely associated with the establishment of a variety of churches and chapels in Parkgate and were pioneers in the Building Society movement. They were very important in the development of housing in Holly Bush, Aldwarke Road and Hall Street.

Opposite: Verdon Coucom in the 12 inch bar mill of the BSC steelworks in Parkgate on its closure in 1975. The mill was originally commissioned in 1935 and 'Verdi' had a very close association with it as he saw it built, he was the first person employed in it and he retired on its last day of production. He spent virtually all his working life at Park Gate steelworks, 49 years in all. For the last 17 years of these he was a furnaceman. When first in production in 1935 the mill's average shift output was 42 tonnes; this had risen to 126 tonnes at its closure. As with many other workers Verdi's family connections with the Park Gate steelworks stretched back a long way, his father Lionel having worked there for 50 years.

Joseph Oxley was closely associated with the manufacture of cast and shear steel in Parkgate. Shown here between 1865 and 1875, he died in 1886 following a stroke. The firm of Messrs W. Oxley and Company had been established by his father in the 1820s when he took over Walker's steelworks at Parkgate. He lived at Alwarke House, close to the River Don, and his obituary describes him as having 'an unassuming and genial social nature'. He left a widow and seven sons and was buried in Rotherham Cemetery.

Above: Kilnhurst Colliery from the air, *c.* 1938. Kilnhurst Pottery was located in the top left hand corner of the site as seen here, just inside the Rawmarsh parish boundary. Large scale mining in this area started originally with the Thrybergh Hall Coal Company sinking a shaft around 1858. This was bought by the Charlesworths ten years later and developed further. The pit that developed here eventually became known as 'Bob's 'Oile'.

Opposite: Many of the residents of Church Street, Rawmarsh are shown round the opening to a small coal pit dug in 1926 during the General Strike. Such community action helped local people to cope with the privations of the strike. Unfortunately this pit was of only limited use as it flooded quite quickly, probably due to the springs that rose in the High Street cemetery nearby. The canary in a cage, vital for such an operation, is shown on the left. Families represented in the photograph include the Jones', the Frosts, the Vaughans, the Tates, the Coopers, the Pearces, the Philips, the Brothertons and the Cawthornes. All these families lived in Church Street at the time, some in the two blocks of back-to-back houses near the top. At this time and earlier many residents would have kept hens or a pig close by.

Rod, Clive, Diana and James Crossland and three of the foundry workers stand outside the Crossland's Foundry in Foundry Street, Parkgate in the early 1960s. The foundry was originally set up late in the nineteenth century but when the Crossland family bought it around 1927 it had reputedly been Turkish baths for some time. In their time there the Crosslands produced decorative metalwork for the gates at the end of Downing Street and for the Tower of London. They produced the cross that stands above St Joseph's Catholic church, Green Lane and, more mundanely, many of the drain grates on the Monkwood estate. The foundry is still operational but no longer owned by the Crossland family.

Chemical Cottages in Birchwood shortly before their demolition. These isolated buildings are shown on the 1854 Ordnance Survey map as Birch Wood Works (Chemical), beside a small pond. Here the White family produced charcoal and wood-naptha for several Sheffield firms for part of the nineteenth century.

Women working in the Park Gate iron and steelworks during the Second World War. A shortage of male labour, as a result of the demand of the armed forces, necessitated the recruitment of women for unusual occupations. The First World War had had a similar, if less widespread, effect and enhanced enormously the drive for women's emancipation.

A mixing furnace at Park Gate iron and steelworks in the 1920s. The works developed close links with the growing motor vehicle industry providing steel for chassis frames, brake drums, wheel hubs and axle housing.

Sir Charles Stoddart held some of the most important executive positions in the Park Gate ironworks in the second half of the nineteenth century. He began his career there as a junior clerk having moved from London. In 1871 he lived in Park Gate House but by 1881 had married Fanny and moved into Granby House on Aldwarke Road. He went on to be Mayor of Rotherham and in 1907 was elected Freeman of the Borough, the first ever. He died in 1913 and was laid to rest after a huge crowd attended his funeral procession.

Warren Vale early in the twentieth century with one of the numerous collieries that had been sunk in this immediate area shown to the left. The first edition of the one inch Ordnance Survey map of the late 1830s showed the three pits at Warren Vale as 'Rawmarsh Colliery'. The Victoria Pit here was begun in 1837 and a tramway carried coal from here down to the River Don at Kilnhurst. A major explosion in 1851 killed 51 miners at Warren Vale and this was followed by another disaster in 1874 when 23 miners died. Shadrock Pearce, who started work there at the age of eleven, had a lucky escape – his eyebrows were burnt off.

Aldwarke Main was being operated by John Brown and Company Limited at this time, *c.* 1900. The company also owned Carr House Colliery on the Rotherham to Greasbrough road having bought both in 1873. In the 1890s Aldwarke produced 2,000 tons of coal a day and employed over 2,000 men and boys. Aldwarke's 'Gas Coal' was well known over a large area.

The pit arch and prop department of the Park Gate iron and steel company, Parkgate, *c.* 1923. There was a very close relationship between the two biggest local industries, the pits supplied the coal to the works to fuel the furnaces (as coke) while the works supplied pit arches and props to the mines to enable them to develop. This department lay beside the junction of Broad Street, Taylor's Lane and Rotherham Road.

Hawley Street close to the Horse and Jockey public house and the site of Low Pottery, *c.* 1950. The street name celebrates the Hawley family who had a major role in the development of the pottery industry locally. William Hawley founded Top Pottery and his son, George, took over Low Pottery in 1859. He lived close by in Pottery House in Dale Road and this later became the Horse and Jockey Inn.

Frank Godfrey, Verdon Coucom and Ron Ashwood at the lighting of the Thrybergh Bar Mill Furnace for the first time in 1973.

The demolition of the two blast furnaces beside Aldwarke Road took place in 1976. They had operated on this site for over seventy years. It was a momentous occasion for the steelworkers and a great opportunity for local photographers!

Bert Oliver on his traction engine in the first decade of the twentieth century. Bert owned Ryecroft Farm (close to St Nicholas Road) and was also a building contractor. He donated the land on which St Nicholas church was built. He was a very competent joiner even into his eighties when he put the wooden seat in Walker Scales' shop.

A view of haymaking on Greasbrough Tops near Westfield Cottage early in the twentieth century. In the background the church of St Mary's stands out prominently as well as the High Street cemetery next to the churchyard. The terraced houses of Church Street can be seen running downhill from the church towards the parish boundary between Rawmarsh and Greasbrough. The stream known as the Old Sough forms the exact boundary here. The agricultural scene serves as a reminder that, despite the prominence of industry in Rawmarsh and later Parkgate, from as early as the eighteenth century, it took place within an active farming framework. In the seventeenth century, Camden, a renowned traveller, wrote of Rawmarsh 'It is famous for earthenware and for the white wheat its fields produced'.

Four

In the News

The residents of Stanley Street, Parkgate celebrate the end of the First World War. The boy standing in the road as if he is rehearsing for the O.K. Corral is a young Walter Hamstead. Note the little boy to the left, whose bowed legs suggest he suffered from rickets. Living conditions were still very difficult for some of the poorer people locally at this time. The figure hanging from the bunting is a mystery; perhaps an effigy of a Zeppelin pilot!

A memorial card recalling the names of seven colliers who died in the pit cage accident at Aldwarke Colliery on 23 February 1904. Four of the seven were local men from Parkgate or Rawmarsh. A steel hawser, a little over an inch in thickness, raised and lowered the cage into the mine. This hawser broke and caused the cage to fall and embed itself in the sump at the shaft bottom. Peter Rockett, one of the victims, had left his home that morning singing a hymn. He had joined the Parkgate Congregational church only a month previously.

A class at Ashwood Road Board School, Parkgate in 1899, with teacher Miss Smith. From left to right, back row: Benny Moore, Danny Marsden, Reggie Reeder, Sid Faulkner, Freddy Powell, John Allott, Len Scothern, Bernard Bray. Third row: Bob Chantry, Neg Gwillan, Austin Healy, Gud Clark, L. Burton, Chuck Hawke, Wally Taylor, Billy Downing. Second row: Irvin Brotherton, Fatty King, Arty Roebuck, Fatther Binns, Piggy Royston, Cyril Hawley, Cobbler Nelson, Reuben Habs. Front row: Chubby Dyer, Joey Downing, Sid Small, Billy Wileman, Leonard Burton, Mick Ensor, Alan Hiskin. Freddy Powell on the back row died in the incident described next.

In January 1905 four people drowned in an ice accident at Bratley's or Brick Pond behind the Little Bridge Inn on Rotherham Road, Parkgate. Those who died were among a small group of spectators standing on the ice watching the skaters. In all seven people fell into the water but three were rescued. Three teenage girls from Rotherham drowned along with Fred Powell, a young lad from Goosebutt Street.

A Swinton and Mexborough tram is stationary outside Victoria Park with its crew posed as if for a recruitment poster! These trams seem to dominate photographs of Rawmarsh and Parkgate from the first three decades of the twentieth century. The bus garage on Dale Road is still commonly referred to as the 'Tram Sheds'.

Ernest 'Kuftee' Evans in his army uniform while serving in the 2nd/5th Battalion of the Yorks and Lancs Regiment in the First World War. He was awarded the Military Medal for his actions in the Battle of Cambrai on 20 November 1917. He advanced across no man's land encouraging his colleagues by dribbling a football. According to his Company Quartermaster-Sergeant he 'advanced almost into a German position where there was still a machine gunner active'. This was a 'typical example of his bravery'. He lost his arm in the following week to an explosive bullet. After the war he worked for Rawmarsh Urban District Council. His exploits are celebrated in the Yorks and Lancs Regimental Museum in Rotherham.

Allan Purseglove and Emily Purseglove (*née* Lawrence) with their children, Allan and George. Allan, shown here during the First World War, was a lance-corporal in the King's Own Scottish Borderers. He was killed shortly after landing in France for the first time.

Albert Lilley, born in Lilley's Yard, Rawmarsh High Street in 1896, served in the Royal Artillery during the First World War.

Harry Bailey signed up for the army towards the end of the First World War; he was 17½ years old at the time. He joined the Dragoons Regiment and was trained to ride horses but fortunately the war ended before he was called to active service. He was demobbed in 1919.

On the night of the 19 July 1926 this group of ex-servicemen erected the 'Little Cross' (which they surround in the photograph) at the top of Rawmarsh Hill on the land set aside for a war memorial. Numerous collections had been held to pay for a more fitting tribute to the fallen of the First World War but these ex-servicemen felt that the organisers locally were 'dragging their feet'. The cross was made in Low End, Parkgate and erected in circumstances of the strictest secrecy at midnight. Guards were posted at either end of Parkgate and Rawmarsh to warn of any possible disturbance. The participants were sworn to secrecy and for most of the remaining twentieth century local people refused to speak of it. Recent enquiries have finally revealed some identities – Clifford Ainley being on the far right of the back row. In the middle row, second left is ? Hancock, the third left ? Hudson and the furthest right Fred Ainley. The front row includes Harry House seated just to the left of the cross with ? Topham second from the right and P.C. 'Bobby' Sowery furthest right.

More recently, this photograph was discovered in the British Legion hut on Rockcliffe Road, Rawmarsh. It includes some of those shown in the more famous photograph but not all and there are one or two different faces. 'Friendly' Smith is shown in the back row fourth from the left with Clem White in the front row second from the right. Although the setting is similar the photographs were not taken at the same time as one or two of those in both photographs wear different clothes. An anonymous letter sent to the *Rotherham Advertiser* in 1939 (signed J.H., O.S., H.H., C.A.) referred to the original incident and stated that of the six people who actually put up the cross, four were still living in Rawmarsh (presumably those initialled), one had died and one had left the area. It mentions that the 'Little Cross' was then 'unfortunately buried within the boundary wall of the existing Memorial'. Of the signatory's, three are believed to be 'Ossie' Stevenson, Harry House and Clifford Ainley.

John Francis (Jack) Ryan, soon after the
First World War. He won a Military
Medal at Loos in May 1916. He was a
founder member of the British Legion
and as such is commemorated in York
Minster. He lived at 86 Rawmarsh Hill.

Harold Hamilton was in the Seventh
Battalion of the Royal Scots Fusiliers.
He grew up in the Bear Tree Road area
of Parkgate and won the Military
Medal when involved in a counter-
attack at Loos in May 1916. He was
battalion runner for Lieutenant-
Colonel Winston Churchill and had
close service connections with the
author, Sir John Buchan. He was the
brother-in-law of John Francis Ryan
and died in 1959.

The offices of the Park Gate Iron and Steel Company are shown decorated to mark the end of the First World War. The offices were located in Broad Street and were built early in the twentieth century in the grounds of Park Gate House.

A vast crowd of over 8,000 people clustered around the new war memorial in Rawmarsh that was unveiled in June 1928. The memorial on Rawmarsh Hill was dedicated by Colonel S. Rhodes, Commanding Officer of the 5th Yorks and Lancs Regiment, and Doctor I.H. Burrows, the Bishop of Sheffield. A film of the ceremony is also surprisingly still in existence. An earlier war memorial had been dedicated at Rawmarsh Old Grammar School, Dale Road on Christmas Day, 1920.

Temporary housing in Naylor Street, Parkgate in 1920. As early as 1890 Dr Picken, the Medical Officer for Rawmarsh, was expressing concern at the high population densities in many streets in Parkgate and the consequent health risks. Many single cottages were inhabited by two families in addition to lodgers. Densities of 7.5 people per house were recorded in a few streets. Problems mounted into the 1920s hence the rather desperate measure of utilising railway carriages as homes.

Stone Row, Rotherham Road, Parkgate in 1920. One of the earliest terraces built in the area these houses actually lay just inside the parish boundary of Greasbrough. The area attracted many complaints in the *Rotherham Advertiser* from 1890 onwards referring to the 'piggeries at people's back doors'!

Poor conditions shown at the back of houses on Hollybush Street in 1920. Many of the houses had been built around 1860 by iron workers linked to the local Temperance Societies.

The backs of terraced houses in Sandhill Road in 1920. This photograph was taken by the Rawmarsh Medical Officer of Health to illustrate the possible health hazards. The link between poor living conditions and poor health had been recognised by this time. A major outbreak of enteric fever had occurred in the Rawmarsh and Parkgate area in 1891 and the subsequent report on it by Dr Theodore Thompson highlighted that a poor quality water supply was the cause.

Parkgate and Aldwarke Station on the Great Central Railway shown close to the First World War and dominated by the view of Aldwarke Colliery in the background. In November 1926 at Rawmarsh South Box close to the station a major train crash occurred. In all nine passengers on the 10.10 service from York to Sheffield were killed and six were seriously injured.

Countess Fitzwilliam is introduced to the Stubbin Colliery cricket team, *c.* 1931. Willie Hague is one of the players shown. Up to the end of the eighteenth century the Fitzwilliams played only a small part in the development of Rawmarsh but throughout the nineteenth and into the twentieth century they took centre stage, especially with the development of Old Stubbin, New Stubbin and Warren House collieries.

Rotherham Road infants' school was badly affected by the floods in 1931. The school was established in 1901 and by 1923 had an average attendance of 93. Children at the school lived locally in Stanley Street and Midland Street. Evelyne Longden, a former headmistress, sometimes had to visit local homes to warn parents that pupils had been playing on the railway lines close by.

The early 1930s were marked by a series of floods in the local area and it was the Low End of Parkgate that suffered worst. The same area flooded most recently in November 2000. Much earlier in 1905/06 the low railway bridge shown here on Rotherham Road created problems when the Mexborough and Swinton Tramway Company wished to run open-top double-decker trams under it with a clearance above the car rails of only 5 feet 7$\frac{1}{2}$ inches.

Servicemen manning the barrage balloon station on Mangham Lane, *c.* 1940. Other protection for the steelworks at Parkgate included gun emplacements on Greasbrough Tops that were in action during the German air raid on Sheffield in December 1940.

The motorised barge *Rowland* passes under Aldwarke Canal Bridge on an excursion to celebrate VJ Day in 1945. Working barges such as this were used on special occasions for excursions.

Nora Ratcliffe (left) and Yvonne Concannon (right) dressed up as cowgirls to take part in a special parade in Parkgate to celebrate the coronation of Queen Elizabeth II.

A 'street party' held in the Queen's Hotel on Kilnhurst Road in celebration of Queen Elizabeth II's coronation in 1953. Left to right, back row: Trevor Griffiths, Peter Roden, -?-, Margaret Crawshaw, Cynthia Dunstan. Front row: David Barnes, Pamela Roden, Roger Hart, Alan Hague, Drina Hart, Stuart Thirkell.

The Whitsun Parade on Broad Street passing the corner of Hollybush Street, c. 1900. The float shown has the title 'Basket of Flowers'. In the background the steps of Parkgate Methodist church can be seen.

The Whitsun Parade was a major highlight of Rawmarsh and Parkgate's social year. Some of the tableaux, such as this one of Samson around 1955, were really very elaborate.

The Whitsun Parade rounds the corner of Thorogate en route for Rosehill Park in 1957, led by Harold Johnson, the steward of High Street Methodist church, Harry Bailey and the Reverend Tribbeck, minister at Ryecroft Methodist church. Closely following is the Salvation Army Band leading the first of the Sunday school banners and tableaux.

The Salvation Army's Sunday school float for the Whitsun Parade in the late 1950s. This tableau involving King Herod was a popular theme and is seen mounted on a Hague's 'pop' lorry. This part of Greasbrough Road close to the Commercial Hotel was the traditional starting point for the procession.

Above: Large crowds were attracted to Victoria Park, Rawmarsh each year for the Holidays at Home scheme. Each year towards the end of the scheme prizes were presented and here around 1952 a boy receives a bicycle. The scheme began originally during the Second World War to encourage families to stay at home at holiday time rather than using up precious fuel. 'Is Your Journey Really Necessary?' was a particularly famous slogan from that time.

Opposite: The aftermath of a train crash that occurred on 21 November 1957. A train carrying 600 tons of coal from Thurcroft to Roundwood suffered brake failure and plunged out of control down a gradient at 60 miles per hour. The driver, Thomas Green, leapt from the engine seconds before it crashed into an emergency air shaft for Silverwood Colliery. Miraculously he received no more serious injuries than abrasions to his hands and face.

The formal opening of the Monkwood School on Saturday 2 July 1960. Third from the left in the front row is the new headmistress, Evelyne Longden. The ceremony was conducted by W.M. Hyman, chairman of the West Riding County Council. Prayers were led by the Reverend C. Richardson, rector of Rawmarsh.

Ernie Allen, Peter Barnfield, Arthur Outram, David Jackson and Edgar Rodgers with the shrouded Rawmarsh churchyard cross on its removal from the south side of the parish church in 1959. Edgar Rodgers was highways superintendent for Rawmarsh Urban District Council and David Jackson was his deputy. The cross, most recently dated to the second half of the twelfth century, was removed with great difficulty because of its great weight and transferred across the road to be stored in a shed in the council yard. Here it lay for over eight years before it was decided in 1967 to re-erect the cross-shaft inside the church at the west end, where it would be protected from the weather. The cross has been described as Anglo-Saxon in the past but the design of pellets and simplified acanthus at the top of the shaft do not appear before the twelfth century and so point to its Norman origins. Even so its antiquity is unmatched by any other surviving piece of the fabric of Rawmarsh.

Five
Are You Being Served?

Walker Scales (Snr) stands in the centre of this group in New Street, Rawmarsh, *c.* 1905. Walker's eldest son, Harold, is shown with him and ? White, ? Billups and ? Kirk. Walker took over Henry Holmes butcher's shop in Dale Road. Some of his time was spent killing and butchering the many pigs that were kept locally in backyards or allotments. The implement resting on the pig was used to shave its skin and pull out its toenails.

The lower end of Broad Street looking towards Rotherham in the mid-1920s. The tall building set forward on the left was the Miners' Institute at this time. It had replaced the Park Gate Temperance Hall that stood there in 1860 and explains the name of the street alongside, Hall Street. The overhead cables for the trams are much in evidence here. On the right hand side Wannop's grocery business and Mason's pawnbrokers can clearly be seen. Also here would have been Tommy Tildesley's chemical herbalist shop. A noted local personality, he is remembered as always wearing a cricket cap. His lobelia balsam and patent liver pills did him no harm as he lived to reach his 100th birthday! Close by was William Longden's prize-winning bakery business, noted for its pork pies.

Looking along Broad Street from Four Lane Ends, c. 1910. Broad Street, with the lower part of Rawmarsh Hill, was the commercial heart of Parkgate with 95 shops or other businesses in 1902 including 14 butchers, 6 drapers and 3 fried fish dealers, a relatively recent retail innovation. Perhaps even more surprisingly there were about the same number of shops and businesses in the streets immediately adjoining Broad Street at this time. The spire of the United Methodist Free church dominates the skyline here. This was built in 1867 at a cost of £2,500 and had seating for 900. It was demolished close to its hundredth anniversary.

This small Co-op shop was at the bottom of Rawmarsh Hill nearly opposite the Methodist church. It is shown here in the early 1900s when it sold mainly meat and game. The young shop assistant on the left is John Bray, who was a commercial traveller later in life. This shop was originally set up by the Masbrough Pioneer Society before it became the Rotherham Co-operative Society.

Ernest Wyatt stands with members of his family outside the off-licence and general store in Claypit Lane, Rawmarsh, *c*. 1898. Ernest, born in 1872, went down the pit at 12 and bought this shop at the age of 23. His wife Kate (*née* Longden) is also shown with their daughters Myrtle and Gladys. The entry to the shop is simply the house's front door and the shop window just the ordinary house window.

The same shop on Claypit Lane with Ernest Wyatt standing outside in the late 1920s. Notice part of the house has been converted into a proper shop with a separate door and a fitted shop window.

Dale Road in the 1950s with the old Crown public house at the end. Walker Scales' van is parked outside his butcher's shop and across the road is the fish and chip shop. The Cocoa Tavern had been opened on this corner with Green Lane in February 1878 with a games room, reading room and cocoa bar. Over 300 members joined in the first few days.

Ellis Ainley, Victor Ainley, Charlotte Ainley, Edith Spick and Jack Spick riding in style, c. 1920. The Ainleys had a furniture shop at Four Lane Ends in Parkgate.

This Co-operative Shop is shown early in the twentieth century and was located halfway up Rawmarsh Hill. The building remains largely unaltered today but houses different retail outlets. Bernard Bray, the warehouse boy, stands to the right of the door. Later he was to be the manager of the Co-op shop in Stocks Lane. The horse and cart shown was for home deliveries and was driven by Dick Ercock.

The present day Queen's Hotel on Kilnhurst Road as it appeared c. 1910. The original building was only completed in the 1870s but by 1901 it had already been found wanting and a new hotel was being proposed.

The old Star Inn in Rawmarsh High Street early in the twentieth century. This building was demolished in 1936. It was stone built and had walls two feet thick. In the past the yard and stables had been used for stabling cattle on their way from distant farms to Rotherham cattle market. When this building was demolished a large well that contained some fourteenth-century pottery was found at its eastern end.

The George Inn on the corner of Taylor's Lane around 1980, shortly before its demolition. John Deighton was landlord here in the 1850s. At that time there was a toll bar close by on Rotherham Road kept by Joseph Turner.

Right: Laura and Ted Watts at the door of their fish and chip shop on Broad Street, Parkgate, *c.* 1930. Seventy years on the shop continues to sell fish and chips. Fried fish dealers first started to appear in the area towards the end of the nineteenth century.

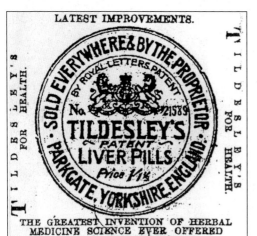

LATEST IMPROVEMENTS.

TILDESLEY'S FOR HEALTH. TILDESLEY'S FOR HEALTH.

SOLD EVERYWHERE & BY THE PROPRIETOR.

BY ROYAL LETTERS PATENT

No. 21589

TILDESLEY'S PATENT **LIVER PILLS** Price 1/1½

PARKGATE, YORKSHIRE, ENGLAND.

THE GREATEST INVENTION OF HERBAL
MEDICINE SCIENCE EVER OFFERED
TO THE SUFFERING PUBLIC.
FOR ALL PEOPLE AT ALL AGES.

They are of greater value to the suffering public than silver, gold, or diamonds, which cannot restore lost health.

Since the invention of TILDESLEY'S PATENT PILLS many sufferers from Diseases have been restored to their usual health, some cases of over three years' standing.

No sufferer need despair if they will only purchase TILDESLEY'S PATENT LIVER PILLS, and take them as directed on each box.

For all the various forms of Liver Complaint, such as frequent Sickness, Acidity, Heartburn, Bilious, Sick Headache, Yellow Jaundice, Giddiness, Dimness of Sight, Pains in the Right Side, Back, or between the Shoulders, Disturbed Sleep, Pains in the Stomach, Indigestion, Loss of Appetite, Wind, Spasms, Swelling after taking Food, Drowsiness, Nervous Trembling, Faintness, Costiveness, Piles, and all those other symptoms which none but a sufferer from a Torpid or Sluggish action of the Liver can describe.

No family should be without TILDESLEY'S PATENT LIVER PILLS, as they are suitable for both sexes.

CAUTION.

The public are requested to notice that the words TILDESLEY'S PATENT LIVER PILLS are engraved on the Label affixed to each box; if not, they are a forgery.

Sold in Boxes at 7½d. and 1/1½ each by all Patent Medicine Dealers; or Post Free for 8 or 14 Stamps, direct from the Manufacturer: THOMAS TILDESLEY, 70, Broad Street, Parkgate, Rotherham.

LOCAL AGENTS:—
MEXBORO': Shields, Pepper.
CONISBORO' and DENABY: Ward.
SWINTON: Jones.
WATH-UPON-DEARNE: Finney.
STAIRFOOT: Ellisson.
HOYLAND COMMON: Ellisson.
HOYLAND and ELSECAR: Matthew.
WOMBWELL: Lambert.
ATTERCLIFFE: J. Watts.
ROTHERHAM: Davy, Pontis, Bolsover, Horsfield, Bingham, Uttley.

Left: Tommy Tildesley, the medical herbalist, advertised his wares in the local press around the turn of the twentieth century. From this advertisement he seemed to be well aware of the art of 'hyping'! He seems to suggest in the advertisement that forgery of his pills was a concern. The list of local agents that completes the advertisement suggests a demand for his Liver Pills over quite an area.

Opposite: Shopkeepers in their long white aprons outside Charles Wannop's grocery business at 104 Broad Street, Parkgate, *c.* 1920. Charles bought the land originally in 1877 and built the shop with a family house over and behind and a hay loft. The street alongside the shop was named after him. When he died in 1900 the business was continued by his son, Charles, and remained a grocery shop right up to about 1960.

Joseph William Coucom standing outside his grocery shop/beer-off at 3 Terrace Road, Parkgate. The window display shows familiar products like Brooke Bond Tea and Fry's Cocoa but also less familiar items such as Tiger Sauce! For much of his working life Joseph was a coal miner.

A general store/grocery shop on Kilnhurst Road, Rawmarsh close to the junction with Claypit Lane, *c.* 1900. The proprietor, Dennis Bailey, stands outside with his wife Catherine (*née* Rodgers). A large number of shops existed at this time in the front rooms of ordinary terraced houses. Many were never fully converted into shops.

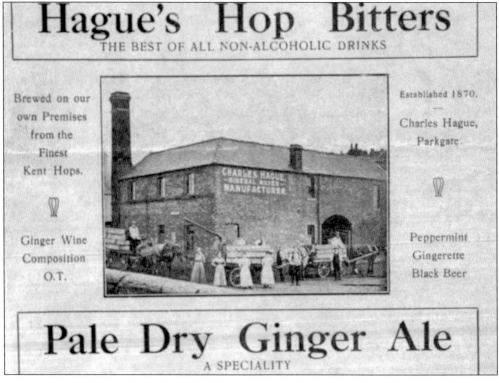

Hague's 'Pop Works' was a feature of the Holm Flatt area of Parkgate for around 100 years. This advertisement was included in a pictorial record of Rotherham from the 1920s. Deliveries were made extensively using horses and carts. The range of products sounds quite intriguing.

Looking down to the bottom end of Stocks Lane, *c.* 1908 with the Crown Inn's Worksop Ales clearly advertised. In 1881 two caravans located in the Crown Inn Yard were each occupied by a professional singer and his family, so it seems that the 'turns' brought their own accommodation! The Congregational chapel is on the left with the general store, later run by Cassie Torr, on the right. The shop's merchandise stretched from buckets and stepladders to bloomers splendidly displayed in the window.

Looking up Stocks Lane from close to the corner with Dale Road in the 1950s. The Co-op shop can be seen on the left with the milk delivery van outside. This was part of the old heart of Rawmarsh swept away by the new shopping centre.

The site of the Rawmarsh shopping centre following the demolition of many of the old buildings on the south side of Stocks Lane and the eastern side of the High Street in the late 1960s. Some historic old houses were demolished as well as substandard Victorian terraces.

The new Rawmarsh shopping centre that was developed from the late 1960s in the area to the east of the High Street. Initially there were great hopes that the centre would revitalize the heart of Rawmarsh as a retail magnet.

Six
Friends and Family

This wedding party is standing in front of Ryecroft infant school in Main Street, c. 1900. The bride is Maud Pugh (one of the notable local builder's family) and the groom is John Edward Caroline. To the left of the groom is the best man, Harry Jackson, and his fiancée, Sarah Caroline. Harry actually went off twice to the Klondike to make his fortune and returned without any great riches. When he suggested a third visit his fiancée left him in no doubt of her opinion!

The infants at St Mary's church school in 1893. At that time the present church hall was used as the school. The teenage girls shown would have been pupil-teachers. This school was closed in 1894 when its 41 pupils were transferred to Dale Road.

Percy Caroline is among the scholars of Rawmarsh Boys Grammar School, Dale Road, shown in the 1890s. The school was established early in the seventeeth century and in 1653 Thomas Wilson provided a house for the schoolmaster and his family. When the house was demolished in 1955 an inscribed piece of stone was removed from the gable end – it read 'This house was built at the proper cost and charges of Mr Thomas Wilson, citizen and cloth-worker of London, 1637'. The teacher shown is 'Gaffer' Blyth who was headmaster to 1901.

The 1936 scholarship class at Rosehill Junior School, Rawmarsh. Their teacher was Mr Holroyd and the headmaster Mr Ingham. From left to right, back row: Irene Colclough, Gordon Stansfield, ? Russel, Alan Senior, William Brown, Stuart Hambleton, Ben Walsh, Harry Schofield, Harold Crawshaw, George Swift, ? Vaughan, Ralph Hutchinson, Decima Penketh. Middle row (sitting): Sheila Parkes, Gertrude Holroyd, Joanne Martin, Molly Beighton, Joan Lilley, Edith Smedley. Front row: Edgar Fearns, Jean Clay, Vivienne Parnham, Brenda Collins and Leonard Elliott.

By the mid-1930s school photographs had moved on. Note how this class group from Netherfield Lane School is much more decoratively arranged than earlier school photos.

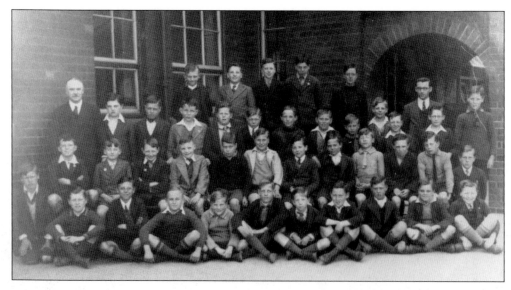

A class of the boys school, Haugh Road in 1935. From left to right, back row: Les Earnshaw, Bill Mitchell, Jack Elliott, Tommy Tinker, Alf Glossop. Third row: John Smith, George Hague, Granville Thorpe, Kenneth Lowe, ? Vickerage, Sid Needham, Arthur Stokes, ? Hatfield, Bernard Hague, Dennis Ward, ? Fletcher, -?-. Second row: -?-, Cyril Bray, Horace Bolton, -?-, Seth Greaves, Roland Dyson, Pete Makin, Jack Webb, ? Hatfield, Sidney McVann, ? Croft, -?-. Front row: -?-, -?-, Jack Allott, Sam Briggs, Brian Moreton, Eric Smallwood, ? Bacon, -?-, H. Cheetham, ? Jenkinson, ? Makin.

A group of children from the newly established Catholic primary school, St Joseph's, that was completed on Green Lane in the mid-1930s. A Catholic church was eventually built in front of the school, but not until the 1950s.

This mixed group of cricketers from around the time of the First World War is linked to Ryecroft Methodist chapel and includes sisters Olga and Ivy Hartley. The photograph may have been taken on the old cricket pitch close behind the Queen's Hotel, Kilnhurst Road. The women hold the bats, had they been playing?

The Bray family of Parkgate, *c.* 1900. Left to right: Ada Bray, John Bray, Charles Bray, Mary-Ann Bray, Bernard Bray, Arnold Bray and Edgar Bray. John, Bernard, Arnold and Edgar were brothers and the children of Charles and Mary-Ann. The Bray family moved into Parkgate in the 1860s from Great Snoring in Norfolk. A sizeable number of people moved from North Norfolk to Parkgate around this time often taking up labouring jobs in the local coalmines. Several were employed to look after pit ponies because of their previous farming experience. Charles found a job as a check-weighman at Aldwarke Colliery interestingly employed by the men rather than the mining company. The Bray family were founder members of the Bethel chapel in Lloyd Street in 1876 and Charles was a local preacher.

A charabanc trip, apparently packed to capacity, outside the Hollybush Tavern, *c.* 1915. The Tavern was at the far end of Hollybush Street from Parkgate. The licensee at this time was Jack Longden. He was born close by in a house used later as part of the old Isolation Hospital. Later his father had a farm near where Netherfield Lane School was built. In 1914 Jack painted a picture of the late King of the Belgians to raise money for the local Belgian Refugee Committee. On Sundays he used to insist on his regulars singing a hymn with him before he served any alcoholic drinks.

A wedding group photographed in Lilley's yard with Ash Mount (which survives today) in the background, *c.* 1908. The group includes a number of the Lilley family. The Lilley's were a very numerous family. Samuel and Eliza Lilley, who lived in Lilley's Yard, had 14 children of whom all but one survived. By 1933 they had 40 grandchildren and 15 great-grandchildren.

A wedding party behind 65 Green Lane, Rawmarsh in 1910, close to where the police station is now located. The wedding was between Carey Steel and a daughter of the Knutton family. The Knuttons had a building and joinery business right up to the late 1960s. Carey was noted for his fine singing voice.

Nurses Brooksbank and Oxley flank the matron, Elizabeth Ellis, at Rosehill Isolation Hospital in 1930. In the foreground is Joan Lilley who was treated here for diphtheria. She survived to pursue a career in nursing herself; some were not so lucky. The death rates of children in the area from the 1870s to the Second World War seem shockingly high when viewed from a modern perspective. Smallpox was still a major concern locally; well over 300 cases were dealt with in an outbreak in 1926.

James Concannon, driver of the ambulance, stands on the left of this group of health workers who were based at the ambulance station in Bear Tree Road, Parkgate in 1950. Things had moved on from 1921 when the area had depended on a horse-drawn ambulance with a horse being hired when required.

The 'urchins' of Pottery Street were rounded up for this photograph in 1919. Pottery Street, which no longer exists, joined Rawmarsh High Street close to the Earl Grey Inn and was named because of the adjacent Top Pottery that consisted of glost kilns, biscuit kilns, dipping houses, slip houses, throwing shops and turning shops. The group includes Jim Evans, Cissie Kendall, Albert Pearce, Hetty Haller, ? Osborne, Lilly France, Jessie Allott, Jane Price, ? Abbott, the Cotterill brothers and the Price twins.

This foursome is ready for tennis in Rosehill Park in 1924. On the left is Elsie Butterworth with Catherine Bailey beside her. The park was the hub of many leisure activities in Rawmarsh at this time.

A coach trip from the Rail Mill Inn on Rotherham Road, Parkgate in the late 1940s. The group, bound for Bridlington, includes Elizabeth Whitehouse and Mary Coe. In the background Parkgate's main gasworks can be seen.

A baby show in Rawmarsh in 1925 with Gladys May Lilley (*née* Doult) proudly holding the winner, Joan Lilley.

A Rawmarsh Congregational church fund-raising 'Bring and Buy', *c.* 1950. The group includes from left to right: Cora Hawkins, Joyce Saxton, Mabel Stones, Brenda Davis, Brenda's daughter, Ben Davis, Margaret Cooper, Mrs Saxton, Mrs Faulkner and Mrs G.M. Lilley.

The Makin family at the wedding of Barbara Humphries in June 1957. Left to right, back row:
Brian Makin, Harry Cotterill, Peter Makin, Jim Evans, Les Lambley, Ruth Makin, Frank
Hillerby, Cyril Stringer, John Humphries. Front row: Marlene Makin, Rosa Makin, Beryl
Makin, Lilian Makin, Agnes Makin, Peter Makin (senior), Harriet Makin, Freda Makin, Violet
Makin, Alice Makin, Ernest Smith.

The opening ceremony at Leonard Green Haulage in 1964. This important local firm was
closely associated with delivering materials to and from the Park Gate steelworks.

Rawmarsh and Parkgate WEA class at Ashwood Road School Parkgate, c. 1945. The older man in the middle of the front row is Sir William Beveridge who played a key role in developing the Welfare State. He gave the main lecture to the class.

The choir and children of Ryecroft Methodist Sunday school celebrating the anniversary of the school in 1956. They are seated in the hall behind the church. This hall (and the folding 'stand' shown) was bought cheaply in Nottingham in 1920 and transported to Rawmarsh where it was erected by members of the church. Fortunately Jack Veitch, the choirmaster, was a skilled joiner! Left to right, front row: Edna Booth, Doris Horner, -?-, Margaret Cooper, ? Brown, Jack Veitch, Nancy Sykes, Edna Harley, Evelyn Cooper, Cathy Purseglove and Sarah Clewley. Standing up on the left is Harry Bailey.

The cast of *Aladdin* from a Rawmarsh Congregational church sisterhood concert, *c.* 1935. Left to right, back row: Alice Lilley, ? Willoughby, ? Jackson, Carlton 'Coltie' Acomb, ? Keay, ? Burford, ? Brameld. Middle row: G.M. Lilley, ? Brameld, ? Faulkner, ? Boughton, ? Tayles, ? Baugh, ? Stones, ? Beaumont, ? Parker. Front row: Lucy Walsh, Flossie Brameld, Eva Brameld, Dorothey Keay, Mamie Tayles, Mary Wainwright.

Visit to the Park Gate works by those who had retired from active service with the company, April/May 1956. From left to right, back row: W. Walker, W. Haines, H. Maiden, J. Williams, W. Brownhill, R. Curry, S. Sparrow, W. Carpenter. Middle row: C. Humphries, W. Underwood, A. Neale, A. Underwood, T. Lowry, J. Caroline, C. Iles, H. Thorpe. Front row: L. Coucom, W. Rising, S. Gill, T. Clayton, A. Bowran, E. Kemp, J. Blyton, W. Longden.

A family group celebrate the golden wedding anniversary of Ellis and Charlotte Ainley in the yard behind Ellis's furniture shop in Parkgate, c. 1927. This shop was later replaced by Woolworth's. Left to right, back row: Eileen Kemp, Clifford Ainley, Edith Ainley, Victor Ainley, Frederick Ainley, Jack Spick. Middle row: Ernest Ainley, Charlotte Ainley, Ellis Ainley, Willis Ainley. Front row: Victor Ainley, Dorothy Ainley, -?-, Charlotte Joan Ainley, -?-. Maurice Ainley is shown on the stool and was obviously added to the photograph later.

A Crossland family group in the early 1950s behind their home at 73 Albert Road, Parkgate. The group includes James Carr Crossland, his wife Winifred, Rod and Clive Crossland. Some of the family worked in the Crosslands Foundry in Foundry Street, Parkgate.

The Crown Inn football team in 1910 at the end of a successful season judging by the trophies. The landlord allowed them to play in the field behind the inn where Greenfields is today. This field was also used as a fairground at this time.

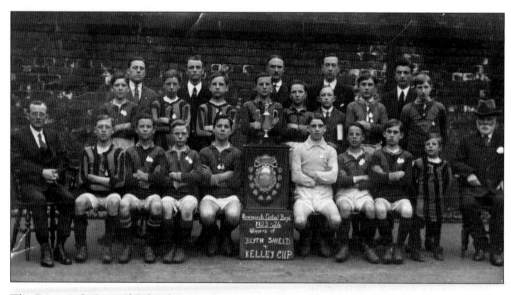

The Rawmarsh Central School team who won the Blyth Shield and the Kelly Cup in 1923/24. Left to right, back row: Mr Sennett, Mr Leadbetter, Mr White, Mr Hensby, Mr Evans (teachers). Middle row: Harry Richardson, Wilmer Burgin, Horace Harrison, Tom Rhodes, Tom Simpson, Frank Sykes (manager), Charlie Robinson, Charlie Hawke. Front row: Councillor Hutchinson, Roland Martin, Sam Astle, John Garritty, Tom Hart, Stan Green (mascot), Mr J. L. Blyth.

The Stubbin Colliery football team who were cup winners, c. 1950. Many of this team also played for Rawmarsh Welfare. From left to right, back row: -?-, Tom Machen, -?-, Harold Pearce, -?-, Fred Cook, Albert Sykes, Charlie Sykes, -?-, Jack Roddis. Front row: Jack Wright, Ted Roddis, Ray Roddis, ? Spooner (manager), Geoff Kirk.

Cliff Wilkinson, captain of Rawmarsh Cricket Club, receives the Yorkshire Council's Victory Cup on 10 August 1950. Rawmarsh defeated Castleford in the final at Barbers Avenue. A large crowd strains to witness the presentation. The club was originally established in 1879 and at one time had over 1,000 members.

The old grammar school building next to the almhouses on Dale Road at Easter 1924. Standing in front of the school is the headmaster Mr Edwin Shelton and his brother Jim.

Ann Elizabeth Coucom, her daughter Florence Cotterill, her two grandchildren Ernie and Bill Cotterill and Miss Kent posing in, rather than driving, a new car in Scarborough, *c.* 1920. As early as 1900 the *Rotherham Advertiser* mentioned that more people in Rawmarsh and Parkgate were taking the opportunity for 'a sojourn at the seaside'. Local trade at that time was described as good with wages improving and so some inhabitants were able to benefit from railway excursions to resorts such as Great Yarmouth and Scarborough. Ann Elizabeth Corbridge had married Joseph Coucom at Christ Church, Parkgate in 1876. Her father, Verdon Corbridge, was a grocer.

Seven
Portraits

Henry Holmes and his wife sitting in the front room of their home at Warren House Farm, *c.* 1900. Henry combined running this livestock farm with his butcher's shops in Rawmarsh and Swinton. His brother Tom also owned a butcher's shop at 90 Broad Street, Parkgate. Another brother ran the Horse and Jockey Inn at around this time.

Bertram Lawrence Ferns sits outside Roe Farm on Dale Road, Rawmarsh at the end of the nineteenth century. His father ran a small dairy farm here and delivered milk in churns to local people. From the age of ten or eleven Lawrence was hired out for agricultural work at Rotherham Statutes Fair.

Edith Mary Ward, c. 1900. She lived in Sunnyside Cottage, High Street and was a well known singer with a fine contralto voice. She often performed at local Sunday schools as well as further afield at venues such as Victoria Hall, Sheffield. There were stables for four horses behind her home and a coach house in which the family's governess cart was kept. Next to the cottage she rented a large garden from the Ecclesiastical Commissioners for the princely sum of two shillings and sixpence.

Canon Frederick Scovell in 1915 shortly after he became rector of St Mary's church, Rawmarsh . His father was a baronet but he was happy enough to visit his parishioners in their kitchens putting his feet up at the fire.

Janet and John William Thorpe with their first child, Edith, during the First World War. John 'Willie' died when he was 33 but his wife, Janet, is still living locally at the age of 108! John 'Willie' was brought up in Pottery Street, his father having come to Rawmarsh from Spalding to work as a traction engine driver. Sadly his brother Charlie died in 1923 when the traction engine he was driving overturned.

The Scales family pose for a portrait just after the end of the First World War. The youngest boys are dressed in sailor suits and an animal skin is a typical addition for a studio photograph of this date. Walker (Snr) is shown in his army uniform with his wife Annie Elizabeth. Their eldest son, Harold, stands at the back with Aubrey, Walker (Jnr) and Victor seated.